Agile Auditing

Steven M. Bragg

For more information about AccountingTools® products, visit our Web site at www.accountingtools.com.

Table of Contents

About the Author

Steven Bragg, CPA, has been the chief financial officer or controller of four companies, as well as a consulting manager at Ernst & Young. He received a master's degree in finance from Bentley College, an MBA from Babson College, and a Bachelor's degree in Economics from the University of Maine. He has been a two-time president of the Colorado Mountain Club, and is an avid alpine skier, mountain biker, and certified master diver. Mr. Bragg resides in Centennial, Colorado. He has written more than 300 books and courses, including *New Controller Guidebook*, *GAAP Guidebook*, and *Payroll Management*. He has also written the science fiction novel *Under an Autumn Sun*, first book in *The Auditors* trilogy.

Steven maintains the accountingtools.com web site, which contains continuing professional education courses, the Accounting Best Practices podcast, and thousands of articles on accounting subjects.

Buy Additional AccountingTools Courses

AccountingTools offers more than 1,500 hours of CPE courses, with concentrations in accounting, auditing, finance, taxation, and ethics. Related courses that you might like include:

- How to Conduct an Audit Engagement
- Internal Auditing Guidebook
- The Audit Risk Model

Go to accountingtools.com/cpe to view these additional courses.

Agile Auditing

Introduction

Agile auditing is a conceptual approach to auditing that provides quicker and more targeted results to clients. It does so by involving clients in the ongoing work of the audit team, and by regularly evaluating its preliminary results and reorienting the audit based on those results. It is intended to be a more-nimble process than the traditional audit approach, resulting in less waste of auditor resources. When conducted well, an auditing team employing agile principles should be able to both identify and respond to risks in short order, rather than grinding through an involved audit program and issuing similar results several months later. In effect, an agile audit is driven by the value provided to the client, rather than the more traditional approach of being driven by an audit plan. In this book, we explore every aspect of agile auditing, including the agile mindset, when to use it, who is on the team, and how projects flow.

The Nature of an Audit

The classic definition of an audit is an examination of an entity's accounting records, as well as the inspection of its physical assets, with the intent of rendering an opinion on the firm's financial statements. This type of audit is restricted by the presence of a lengthy audit program, mandating that a variety of tasks be completed, depending on the nature of the client's system of internal controls. There is little room for an agile audit in this type of carefully-defined work environment.

The situation is entirely different for an internal audit. Internal audits can be conducted over a nearly infinite array of functions, encompassing such matters as fraud detection, internal control assessments, and regulatory compliance. Internal audits are conducted for the benefit of the business, and so essentially cast the internal audit department in the role of an internal consulting department that actively adds value to an organization's operations. It does so by highlighting opportunities for improvement and facilitating changes within the business.

In the context of an internal audit, who is the client? This is the party that gains value from the findings of the audit team. The most common audit client is a department manager, but it may also be a process owner, the board of directors, or a division manager. In short, a client could potentially be anyone operating within a business, or its directors.

As just noted, an internal audit can be directed at virtually any target, such as the controls associated with a company's use of coupons, whether the controls used in a process are interfering with its efficiency, or perhaps whether there is a risk of checks being stolen in the mailroom. In general, audits tend to be focused on either risk identification, compliance, or cost reduction activities. Risk identification covers a vast area, including how an attacker could plant malware in a company's computer systems, whether there is a sufficient separation of duties in the cash receipts function, and how an employee might steal goods from a company warehouse. Given the breadth of possible risk analyses, an audit team may need to bring in outside experts to assist it in risk identification. This is also a concern in the area of compliance, where an expert may need to be brought in to provide advice on such matters as pollution and safety compliance. This is less of an issue with cost reduction, where an audit team with traditional data accumulation and analysis skills is more likely to be able to identify cost reduction opportunities throughout an organization. In short, audit teams may need to take in outside experts in order to provide the greatest possible value to clients, depending on the nature of the engagement.

The Agile Mindset

In order to engage in agile auditing, the auditor must adopt the agile mindset, which avoids any set methodology and instead focuses on getting tasks done in short order. Doing so requires the auditor to identify any uncertainties that may impact the work, and make adjustments on the fly.

The auditor must also work closely with the client to determine what is needed, and how to deliver that information as quickly and precisely as possible. This level of communication is also needed within the audit team; people do not wait for the next scheduled meeting to state their findings, but rather do so at once. This typically results in daily meetings within the team, if not more frequently.

Communications both within the team and with clients also work in the other direction. If someone on the audit team is in need of resources or information, he or she says so at once. Doing so results in the more immediate delivery of whatever is needed, thereby compressing the audit completion date.

High levels of communication also mean that the audit team and client jointly discover that the original goal of an audit may not be relevant to the client, and that a different target should be pursued. This means that an agile audit team should be willing to pivot during an audit – perhaps several times – in order to pursue a more valuable outcome.

Finally, the agile mindset operates within an extremely compressed timeframe, such as one or two weeks. By requiring the team to complete its activities within such a short period, it is forced to weed out any delays that might normally be accepted in its audit processes, such as interminable meetings or waiting weeks for the client to provide necessary data. This results in an intense focus on the elimination or circumvention of all bottlenecks, while highlighting any wait times that need to be compressed.

EXAMPLE

An internal audit manager for Medusa Medical (maker of snake oil therapies) is asked to conduct an audit of the controls used by the company for the receipt and recordation of cash. The cash recordation process is a complex undertaking for the company, since cash may be paid to its traveling salespeople, sent in by check to 20 company locations, or remitted via direct deposit. Given the complexity of the process, it takes the audit manager three weeks to come up with a set of criteria against which the existing controls would be assessed. On the first day of field work, it becomes apparent that no cash receipt controls are being followed anywhere in the company. Because Medusa uses a traditional, highly structured audit process, the audit manager is forced to continue working through the audit program for another six weeks before summarizing her results and presenting them to management.

If the audit had instead been organized as an agile audit, the audit team would have determined just the highest-risk control in this area, conducted tests, concluded that there was a problem, and immediately communicated the issue to management for remediation. The difference between the two approaches is that agile auditing results in a much faster identification of the issue, so that it can be corrected.

The Ideal Agile Auditor

The preceding discussion of the agile mindset suggests what the characteristics of an ideal agile auditor might be. This person is highly participative, being willing to share findings with both the client and other team members throughout the audit. This requirement also implies that an agile auditor have excellent listening skills, in order to pick up the maximum amount of information from the rest of the team, as well as the client.

This person should also be possessed of a significant amount of backbone. This means that the ideal auditor should be willing to question the work of other team members, both in terms of the testing methods used and their interpretation of the results. This characteristic needs to be paired with a significant amount of respect for others, so the auditor's questioning attitude is not perceived as annoying by other team members.

The agile auditor should also be highly self-motivated, being able to both plan for and revise work on a continuing basis. This also means that the person should be comfortable in an uncertain environment, where the work plan at the beginning of the day is not necessarily the one in place at the end of the day.

Comfort with uncertainty also suggests that the ideal agile auditor be willing to innovate, trying new ideas in order to get work done faster. Innovation is an especially useful characteristic when trying to work around a bottleneck; alternative approaches may be needed to find a way forward.

Another characteristic of the ideal auditor is being able to manage his or her time well. This is extremely important during sprints (as discussed later), where tasks must be completed as expeditiously as possible. Those with the best time management skills tend to have an easier time living with less-than-perfect audit results; this is important, since adding on more audit tests in order to confirm a preliminary result can be quite time-consuming, resulting in extended time intervals that cannot be accommodated by the sprint schedule.

A key skill of an agile auditor (as opposed to a characteristic) is being able to engage in data analytics analysis. This means knowing how to analyze the raw data for an entire population in order to draw conclusions. This certainly beats the usual approach of only being able to draw conclusions from a relatively small sample. An auditor can extract more patterns and anomalies from an entire data set, resulting in richer conclusions and more meaningful recommendations for the client.

It is also worthwhile to identify the characteristics of someone who would *not* work well as an agile auditor. This person should not be wedded to a specific audit program, since doing so forces the person to follow a predefined set of steps, even when the preliminary findings point in a different direction. The result is inefficient and prolonged audit work. In addition, this person should not glory in finding mistakes committed by the client; doing so merely makes the client reactive, rather than wanting to assist the team.

When to Use Agile Auditing

When does it make sense to switch over from traditional auditing to the agile approach? There are several situations that may call for its use. Consider the following:

- Audits are taking so long that it has become too difficult to plan a series of audits for the fiscal year.
- The audit manager is concerned that some staff auditors are maximizing their use of the budgeted hours on audits, rather than trying to get actionable findings back to clients as soon as possible.
- The efficiency with which audits are being completed has flattened. There do not appear to be any ways to enhance the efficiency level any further.
- Audits are taking too long, due to a gradual expansion of their scope (known as scope creep).
- Team members are dissatisfied because of reviewer nitpicking of their work-papers; this also prolongs the duration of audits while reviewer notes are cleared.
- There have been complaints from client departments because it takes too long for the internal audit department to initiate a requested audit, and too long to complete it.
- It is taking too long to formulate audit reports, so that recommendations may not be issued to clients until weeks after field work has been completed.
- There is some dissatisfaction among client departments, because they do not see the internal auditing group providing them with enough value. Further, they disagree with the findings and recommendations contained within audit reports.

Any one of the preceding situations can justify the rollout of an agile auditing program. When two or more of these situations are present, there is a strong justification for the switchover.

There is one situation in which agile audits are especially recommended. This is when a business is operating in an environment where new risks are constantly emerging. This is most likely to be the case when an organization is entering a new market or launching a new product line – situations most commonly applicable to an organization that is growing at a rapid pace. In these situations, an auditing team may be assigned a project on short notice, and be expected to return results within a few weeks.

Agile Audit Constraints

The standard constraints that apply to any project are the amount of available time, the cost of the project, and its scope. For example, broadening the scope of a project will likely increase the amount of time and cost required to complete it. This frequently results in cost overruns and greatly extended project durations for most projects, since the scope tends to be relatively fixed. The situation differs for an agile audit, where the duration and cost of the work are fixed; instead, the team decides on the scope of the engagement as it progresses. Under this scenario, the initial scope of the work may change as the team progresses through its investigatory work and revises its view of what constitutes a completed project. As part of this process, the team deals with the highest-risk items first and works on successively lower-risk items until the end of each sprint has been reached. This means that activities focused on lower-risk activities may never be completed, or at least will be held over until an audit team can address them at a later date.

Audit clients love agile audits, because these projects are largely completed on time and within budget. They tend not to be too concerned if the scope of the work turned out to be different from the original request, because clients are involved in the decision-making process as the work proceeds. Since they are involved, they can see the preliminary results that the team has obtained, and so have the best possible view of why scope modifications may be needed.

Members of an Agile Audit Team

There are only a few roles within an agile audit team. In the following sub-sections, we describe the functions of each of these roles.

Product Owner

The product owner defines the work that a team will address, and prioritizes which work items need to be completed first. This prioritization is based on a determination of the value proposition associated with each work item. The product owner presents to the team the vision of what needs to be done, why it needs to be done, and why it will help the client. This is a leadership role, rather than a management role; the product owner presents to the team a vision of what needs to be done, and then lets the team decide how to fulfill the vision.

The product owner also decides when a product has been completed, so that its results can be turned over to the client. In addition, the product owner manages relations with all stakeholders in the work.

The product owner serves as the interface between the client and the audit team. As such, this person represents the interests of the client, and so wants to provide a valuable outcome for the client. To be an effective interface, the product owner must have excellent listening skills. This is needed in order to fully understand the needs of the client, and to understand how the team is dealing with the audit tasks to which they have been assigned. When either party has questions about the progress of the audit, the product owner is in a good position to clarify issues and help everyone decide how to proceed.

The product owner always has some involvement with the audit team, but it varies depending on the phase of the work. This person is most involved during the planning phase of a project, and maintains contact during field work by attending the daily update meetings.

Ideally, the product owner should be the head of the audit team, rather than someone from the client. Taking this approach promotes the independence of the audit team from the client. For example, having the client decide when a project is complete interferes with the independence of the team, especially when field work reveals that the client is engaged in fraudulent activities. In addition, having the product owner come from the audit team ensures that this person is quite familiar with professional auditing standards.

Facilitator (Scrum Master)

Each agile audit team is assisted by a facilitator (sometimes called a scrum master), who essentially acts as the grease that keeps the project moving. This person advises on the correct approach for how to proceed, including the facilitation of all meetings, coaching team members about how to manage their areas of responsibility, and assisting in the removal of bottlenecks. Rather than being a manager, the real goal of a facilitator is to boost the productivity of the team.

> **Tip:** A more senior auditor is typically appointed to the facilitator role, since this person has the most experience with how an audit should be conducted. However, not all senior auditors can be good facilitators, tending to slip out of their new advisory role and into their old management role.

A particular concern for the facilitator is the removal of bottlenecks, since they can destroy a delivery timeline. This person should be skilled at pointing out potential chokepoints, what work will be impacted by them, and discussing possible workarounds with the team.

The ideal facilitator has excellent communication skills, being able to listen carefully to team members and offer advice as needed. When facilitating meetings, the ideal person encourages comments from others, pulling team members into the discussion on a regular basis. Communication also means motivating others – the facilitator should be able to identify instances in which a team member needs encouragement, and provides it as needed.

A further communication skill is to identify when a conflict exists – either within the team or between team members and the client – assess the situation, and assist the parties in minimizing the conflict. This is an especially important skill in an agile team environment, where auditors are typically working closely together to complete work on a tight deadline.

As part of the facilitation process, it is also useful for this person to identify instances in which proposed actions cannot be completed within the audit timeline.

When a team member puts forth an overly generous estimate of how long it will take to complete a task, the facilitator should be willing to question this estimate in order to keep the team working on a realistic set of tasks.

A significant amount of backbone is also required in this role. The facilitator should step in whenever a change in scope is proposed, to heighten awareness of the impact of this change on the audit timeline. The facilitator must also be willing to cut off outsiders who attempt to interfere in or influence the work of the audit team.

Team Member

The single most unique aspect of the team member position is that this person is self-managing. They have the authority to determine how they will get work done, develop a timeline, and conduct tasks. Where needed, team members may review the work of others or provide training as needed to fulfill the immediate work targets.

The most successful team members are those who can accurately estimate how much time it will take to complete tasks, manage their time to get work done as promised, and work independently on some tasks and collaboratively on others.

> **Tip:** It can be especially difficult for a more junior-level auditor without much experience to keep track of the tasks to which he or she is committed. Successful team members can overcome this issue by working through a daily list of priority tasks, so that the most critical items are completed first. Another option is to understand when your energy levels are highest, and complete the most difficult tasks during those times, leaving more routine activities for lower-energy periods.

> **Note:** There are few titles within an agile audit team. Nearly everyone works on similar tasks, and are responsible for their own work. The team jointly decides who will work on which tasks, and as such is self-governing. Thus, the organizational structure is extremely flat.

Many auditors have a difficult time performing within an agile audit team, because they are not accustomed to the absolute lack of hierarchy. Instead, they need to be able to rely on the unique skills of the team – as a group – to jointly achieve the goals of the audit.

The Value Proposition of an Agile Audit

Before beginning an agile audit, it is essential to develop a value proposition for the project. Ideally, it should be tightly linked to the strategy of the organization, while also meeting one of the following needs:

- It creates a competitive advantage for the business
- It enhances the customer experience or minimizes a negative one
- It enhances the goods or services being provided by the business
- It meets a specific customer need

- It minimizes bottlenecks
- It reduces an identified risk

Within the previous considerations, remember that the primary goal of an agile audit is to assess the controls for the highest-rated risks. These are the risks that impact the achievement of an organization's objectives.

EXAMPLE

As an example of how a controls assessment can be combined with one of the needs described in the preceding bullet points, an audit team finds that there is a serious disconnect between a firm's field servicing teams and its parts reordering group. The company provides field servicing for home gym equipment, such as elliptical trainers and treadmills. Field servicing personnel submit orders for broken or worn-out parts to the firm's purchasing department, which is having trouble tracking the status of these orders with suppliers. The result is a negative customer experience (the second bullet point noted above) as well as a risk of lost revenue, since the company does not bill its customers until replacement parts have been installed.

An agile audit team conducts an analysis and determines that there are no controls at all over the placement of orders with suppliers, or the subsequent monitoring of these orders. It recommends five new controls to ensure that orders are placed in a timely manner and monitored to ensure that customer-owned equipment is made operational again as soon as possible.

If an adequate value proposition cannot be achieved, then it would be better to hold off on conducting an audit, on the grounds that the audit team's resources would be better applied elsewhere. Because of this tight focus on the value proposition, agile audit teams tend to generate a high return on investment (ROI). This triggers a positive feedback loop, which is that the high ROI causes clients to demand more services from the internal audit department.

> **Note:** A tight focus on the value proposition means that an agile audit is likely to focus on just a single risk area. This can be a jarring switch for auditors accustomed to a traditional audit that encompasses every possible risk associated with a client area. If a risk area is assessed as having low risk, then it is not audited. The key point is that agile audits are *precisely* targeted at the biggest risk areas; lesser risk areas are not addressed until audits have been completed for higher risk areas.

The Agile Audit Project Backlog

A traditionally-managed internal audit department typically compiles a list of audits to be completed during the upcoming fiscal year, obtains funding for them, and then issues a schedule for the year, noting the order in which audits will be completed. This is not the case when agile auditing is used. Since the information found during any audit can trigger an immediate change in priorities, it is quite likely that the audit schedule will be juggled in an unpredictable manner throughout the year.

Consequently, it makes little sense to plan with a formal audit schedule. Instead, an internal audit department that employs agile auditing simply maintains a backlog of prospective projects, from which it schedules audits only for the immediate future – perhaps the next month. It picks the next audit projects for the short-term schedule from the backlog, based on the information gleaned from its most recent audits. The period covered by this short-term schedule is based on the amount of lead time that an organization needs before an audit can be started. Smaller organizations can typically work with quite a short-term schedule, while larger and more complex ones may require a longer planning interval, such as one or two quarters.

EXAMPLE

The engineering department of Milford Sound, maker of fine audio equipment, has developed a new speaker system for stadium concerts that generates remarkably resonant sound. Unfortunately, these speakers require large amounts of yttrium, which is a mineral classified as a rare earth. It is almost entirely mined in China, with much smaller mines located in India, Brazil, and Malaysia. Relying on China for yttrium presents a political risk for the company, since this source could be cut off at any time.

Given these facts, it would be appropriate for an agile audit team to conduct a review of the purchasing department's efforts to acquire yttrium from one of the other three supplying countries. The team would not look at any other processes within the purchasing department, since it is focused solely on the political risk associated with the acquisition of yttrium.

In a larger business, it may make sense to maintain a separate project backlog for each business unit or risk category. For example, a purveyor of retail goods might maintain a separate backlog for each of its distribution channels – one each for its Internet store, retail chain operations, and distributor operations. Alternatively, a power plant operator might maintain separate project backlogs for regulatory risks and another for its strategic risks. Typically, a single product owner is assigned to each of these backlogs. Doing so allows one person to specialize in a cluster of risks, which makes the person better able to discern which risks are more in need of attention from an agile audit team.

> **Note:** Some projects may have such low risks associated with them that they remain parked low on the backlog list. As such, they may never be addressed at all.

The Agile Project Flow

An agile audit is broken up into a series of increments, known as *sprints*. Each sprint contains a specific increment of work that must be completed by team members, as decided upon during an initial planning meeting. This planning meeting includes the following activities:

1. The product owner discusses the project from the perspective of the client and provides background information that pertains to the project. This person also notes specifically how the audit's outcome can add value to the organization.
2. The facilitator works with the audit team to define the goal of this sprint, as well as the tasks that they will address during the upcoming sprint. This includes a discussion of the resources required, and who will perform each task. The group also decides upon the acceptance criteria that it will use to decide when tasks have been completed.

> **Tip:** If key resources are not available, this issue needs to be brought up during the initial planning meeting. If there is no way around a resource blockage, then the audit should not start until the resource is available.

The audit client may participate in this planning meeting in order to provide insights into what the team can expect to encounter. The client may also describe existing controls and offer opinions about how they may be tested.

EXAMPLE

The internal audit department of Arbitrary Outcomes (which provides lottery consulting services) is asked to conduct a review of the firm's controls over fixed assets. The audit team's initial expectation is that controls will need to be examined for the dozens of laptop computers issued to the firm's consultants, which are routinely taken on road trips to visit state lottery commissions. As part of the initial discussion of the project with management, the team learns that management has a high risk tolerance for this investment, since it replaces all laptops once every two years. Given management's tolerance level, the team decides to skip all tests of controls over the laptops, focusing its attention elsewhere on risk areas that are of more interest to management.

As the work progresses, the team jointly examines and interprets the results of all tests conducted; this approach minimizes waste in the testing process, and also identifies any errors that might have crept into a test. In addition, the results of one test might indicate the need to alter the remaining tests that are planned for the sprint. For example, if a test of a firm's software discovers a bug, then the team might add a new task, which is to investigate with the client the ramifications of the bug and its plans to eliminate it.

Over the course of a sprint, the team meets for a short period of time (such as 15 minutes) each day, with the team facilitator running the meeting, to provide updates and give feedback, with the intent of enhancing communications within the team. It can be useful for the group to maintain a project status board for these meetings, so that there is a visual display of the current status of all tasks. A simple display format is to list each task as either to-do, currently in process, or complete.

> **Tip:** To promote consistency, hold the daily meeting at the same time every day.

When engaged in a sprint, team members usually focus on only a small number of tasks, which avoids having to manage multiple activities concurrently. This narrow focus makes it easier to complete tasks, which in turn makes it easier to identify problem areas. Also, the avoidance of concurrent activities makes it easier to avoid having any hanging activities at the end of a sprint that will require additional work to complete.

If the initial results of a sprint do not lead the team toward its expected goal, the project leader can elect to save resources by cutting off the remainder of the time devoted to the current sprint. The team then meets to reevaluate what it should be doing, and formulates a new sprint. This approach can save a significant amount of time during an audit.

At the end of each sprint, the team meets with the client to evaluate its results. The outcome of that meeting will decide the nature of the next sprint, for which a new increment of work will be devised. This ongoing series of sprints can result in several shifts in the direction of the audit, depending on the results that are found. Also, based on the information obtained in the last sprint, the client can decide which goals now have the highest priority, which also drives the direction of the next sprint.

Note: A further advantage of the iterative nature of agile auditing is that any misunderstanding of the client's requirements will be uncovered by the end of the first sprint, rather than at the end of a traditional, lengthy audit. A correction can then be made, without any additional audit resources being wasted.

The team may also engage in a retrospective analysis at the end of each sprint. This analysis is intended to point out lessons learned, to decide which actions worked well and which other ones are in need of improvement. If the team engaged in any non-value-added activities, they can be flagged at this time and excluded from the next sprint. This ongoing analysis is useful for increasing the efficiency of each successive sprint.

Note: Given the high speed with which agile audits are conducted, it is common to run into imperfect audit situations where there are errors or some degree of uncertainty regarding outcomes. These situations are accepted in the agile audit environment as a common side-effect of the increased project speed. It can be difficult for a more hidebound auditor who insists on audit perfection to work within this environment.

Training Within an Agile Audit Team

In a traditional auditing environment, auditors with special expertise are scheduled onto an audit to conduct a specific task, after which they roll off the project. This can be a problem when agile audits are being scheduled within a short time frame, since it may not be possible to bring in specialists on such short notice. To get around this problem, agile audit teams may call upon a knowledge expert from the client for assistance. Another option is to limit the types of projects that will be assigned to a specific audit team to items that they are capable of handling without any specialist assistance. This can be done by letting each team select those audits that they feel they are technically capable of handling. A final option is to form audit teams that are comprised of a mix of the skills that will most likely be needed; thus, people with a solid knowledge of (for example) IT, regulatory requirements, and operations are always available. In general, bringing in experts for a limited period of time to work on an audit is considered suboptimal; the other solutions presented here are preferred.

> **Tip:** When an audit team is formed that already has a mix of the skills most likely to be needed, it makes sense to keep the group together for as long as possible through a series of audits, to keep from losing necessary technical skills. This approach also results in a more efficient team over time, as they learn how to work together better in completing audits.

The Client Interface

When engaged in an agile audit, there is certainly pressure to complete the work associated with a sprint within a very short time frame. Doing so requires a significant amount of assistance from the client. This can be a problem, since the client also has to conduct its normal day-to-day business activities. Consequently, it can make sense to schedule these types of audits during periods when there is a natural slowdown in business transaction volume, so that client personnel can reasonably be expected to break free from their normal work. If the audit must be conducted during a busy period for the client, then inquire as to whether there are slow periods during the day when client personnel would be better able to provide assistance. In cases where it is simply not possible to obtain much client time to help with an audit, the only remaining solution may be to limit the scope of work to match the amount of available client support.

> **Tip:** Try to position the audit team at the client location for the duration of each audit. Doing so minimizes the amount of travel time, both for the audit team and the client.

A client interface issue that is decidedly unique to agile auditing is being willing to share the audit program with the client. This is not as sacrilegious as might initially appear to be the case. After all, audit tests are done on a sampling basis, so who knows which transactions might be selected? If the client wants to comb through the entire population of transactions in advance and clean them up, then so be it – the result will be extremely clean test results, with no findings or recommendations from the auditor.

It is also quite useful to conduct testing in conjunction with the client. By having the client in the same room with the auditors, the audit team can verify that the sample pulled by the client was the one actually selected by the auditors. In addition (since the client is still there), the auditors can quiz the client about any exceptions found, thereby completing all testing in one pass. There are no delays in waiting for responses from the client, because the client is assigned to the audit team during the testing process. While this is a terrifically efficient approach to testing, it will require dedicated client time – which brings us back to the first paragraph of this section, scheduling the audit to maximize available client time.

A further benefit of having clients directly involved as a respondent in the testing process is so that they can see how the testing process works. Since they are working through the investigation of each exception found alongside the auditors, it is quite likely that they will be in full agreement with the auditors when any uncleared exceptions are eventually reported back to the client as findings. In addition, the client can educate the auditors about how to understand the samples being investigated, which adds to their knowledge base – and may be of use during the next sprint that is associated with a related topic.

A parting thought on the client interface is that working with an agile audit team actually requires much less work for the client than would be the case with a traditional audit – even though the client needs to be with the audit team during the testing portion of its sprint work. There are several reasons for this. First, the client no longer has to spend time formulating email responses to auditor questions, since all questions have already been answered. Second, the client and auditor can discuss exactly what information needs to be collected in cases where there appears to be an exception, rather than having the client go off and collect more information than is actually needed. And finally, the client already knows what the auditors' findings will be, and so does not have to waste time formulating a response to object to any of them.

Priorities of an Agile Audit Engagement

In agile auditing, projects are prioritized based on their importance (i.e., risk), as well as on the readiness of both the client and the audit team to conduct the work. If the readiness level for a proposed project is too low to justify starting an audit now, then actions are taken to bring in the necessary resources. For example, if an audit team needs to interact regularly with a client's management reporting software developer, then the audit is planned around the work schedule of the developer. In short, project importance levels and resource bottlenecks drive when an agile audit will be conducted.

Outcome of the Agile Audit

The success of an agile audit is judged entirely by the value of the product provided to the client. Given this definition, an audit team should be willing to pivot as many times as necessary in its pursuit of the most valuable outcome from the perspective of the client. Conversely, unwaveringly following the original project goal and providing exactly what the client originally asked for may eventually result in a failed project rating, if the team could have more profitably diverged mid-course to pursue a better objective.

EXAMPLE

Rambling Dirt, maker of conveyors for gravel pit operations, has traditionally conducted an audit of its billing practices once every three years. It is now time for another audit, so the audit manager dusts off the last audit program for billings, and decides to duplicate an examination of the risks identified three years ago, which were the risks of not issuing a billing at all and of not ensuring that billings are sent to an authorized person at the correct customer location.

However, the economy has recently taken a sharp downward turn, resulting in negative cash flows for the company and a significant amount of bad debt. In light of the immediate need to improve profits, the audit team questions whether a review of the same old risks will provide much value to the business. Instead, they suggest a pivot to the credit function, where they will instead examine the risk of issuing credit to customers that are in no financial condition to pay the company. This represents better value for the client.

By promulgating the use of pivots, we do not mean to imply that the client should be surprised by the delivery of a report that focuses on a different subject area. Instead, the client should be included in (and agree with) all discussions of prospective team pivots, so that it is in agreement with the various twists and turns that the team may elect to go through over the course of its engagement.

Administrative Overhead in an Agile Audit

Many of the administrative overhead tasks that can bog down a traditional audit can be either scaled back drastically or eliminated entirely in an agile audit. For example, there is no need to track the time worked by each team member. They may switch among a variety of tasks on short notice, so there is no point in precisely tracking where their hours were spent each day. In addition, there is little point in developing a budget that itemizes the hours to be expended on each task, so there is no reason to track actual hours worked in order to compare them to a budget that does not exist.

Another area in which to scale back administrative overhead activities is in the handling of workpapers. In a traditional environment, an audit team will compile workpapers and then subject them to a series of reviews to ensure that every possible issue has been dealt with, and that the workpapers are internally consistent. This is not the case in an agile audit, where the entire thrust of the team's efforts is focused on delivering findings to the client as soon as possible. This means that the polishing of workpapers will lag well behind the presentation of findings to the client – at which point there are few good reasons to continue examining and revising the workpapers.

There are other reasons to downplay the need for workpaper reviews. First, because of the short duration of each sprint, the complexity of each separate sprint is relatively low, thereby reducing the need for a detailed review. Second, the client (an expert in the subject matter) is present when workpapers are being written, and so can point out issues at that time. And finally, the audit team works together, and so the creation of workpapers is a joint effort in which everyone takes part; this means that the workpapers are, in effect, being reviewed by one's peers.

In an agile environment, the review of audit tests is conducted as soon as they have been completed, so that the associated workpapers are updated almost immediately. This is more efficient than subjecting the workpapers to a review only after all audit work has been completed, when team members are distracted by other tasks or may even have moved on to other audit projects.

> **Tip:** It is especially worthwhile to minimize the time spent on workpapers when you consider that workpaper preparation time can take twice as long as the time spent conducting tests.

> **Note:** If an agile audit team pares back its administrative overhead activities, then what sorts of work should it be doing? The main emphasis will be on the identification and assessment of risks, as well as the formulation of improved controls and processes that will reduce costs.

Agile Audit Reporting

The findings of an agile audit team are short and very much to the point. This is not an elaborate production that goes through multiple rounds of editing before being presented to the client, as is the more traditional approach. The reason for the difference is that the client has already been involved in the audit process – possibly every day – and so is already familiar with the findings, and may already have started working on remediation activities to correct any issues found. In this environment, developing a lengthy report is a waste of everyone's time and money. Instead, the focus of the report may be on nothing more than a list of findings and recommendations. That being said, the audit team should go over the contents of its final report with the product owner prior to delivering it to the client. This meeting is useful for the product owner, who now knows which sprint tasks were completed, and so can be removed from the backlog.

> **Note:** The product owner does not approve the audit team's final report.

Benefits of Agile Auditing

Now that we have addressed the essential aspects of agile auditing, we can itemize the benefits of this approach. One benefit is that it encourages self-management in a fast-paced environment. This allows audits to be completed much more quickly, with a focus on providing the highest-value findings and recommendations to clients as soon as possible. It also encourages constant interaction with clients; their inclusion in the audit process makes it easier to keep the audit team focused on the needs of the client, and also provides clients with early access to audit findings while audit work is still underway.

An agile audit can be a freewheeling environment. Rather than assigning the standard work to a team member that would normally be associated with that person's job title, the team is free to allocate work amongst the group as they see fit. This environment gives auditors the opportunity to gain skills and experience more rapidly than would be the case in a traditional audit environment.

A unique advantage of agile auditing is that the audit team is encouraged to discuss risks with the client as soon as an audit begins, rather than conducting an "ivory tower" analysis of what the most critical risks are most likely to be. The agile approach allows for the immediate identification of key risks, which accelerates the conduct of the audit and concentrates attention on the examination of the most important controls.

An essential benefit is that it is simply easier to manage projects in an agile environment. Each member of the team reports his or her progress every day, so it is immediately obvious when planned work is not being completed on time; the fast reporting makes it easier to make adjustments to the remaining amount of planned work. Also, and again because of the daily progress reporting, team members can publicize any bottlenecks or other issues encountered, so that they can be addressed as soon as possible. And finally, any work not completed at the end of a sprint is simply rolled into the work backlog, to be dealt with in a future sprint. One way or another, the current sprint is complete; it is not dragged out in order to deal with a few residual tasks.

To build on the last point, the use of a project backlog makes it easier to keep a project's scope reasonable. If an audit team spots a new issue that might require additional work, it is simply appended to the current backlog, rather than being included in the current audit – which would increase its scope and likely prolong the audit.

Yet another benefit is that a review process is included at the end of each sprint. This gives the audit team time to reflect on what went both right and wrong during the last sprint, which in turn can lead to suggestions for how to conduct the next sprint in a more efficient manner. Compare this approach to that of a traditional audit, where there may be a review meeting at the very end of an audit – if at all – when most team members can barely remember any issues that arose during the early stages of the audit.

Another benefit of agile auditing is a strong focus on assisting clients with their business objectives. This means that the investigation of risks that are linked to business objectives receive the highest priority from an audit team. If the risks being investigated are not linked to any business objectives, then the audit team should not be investigating them.

A further benefit is that the final report can be completed and delivered extremely fast. Since the audit team has been working in close collaboration from the start, it can jointly assemble the report immediately after all audit work has been completed. The group can also jointly review the report, so that it can be released to the client the same day. In addition, clients are much less likely to challenge the findings and recommendations of the audit team. This is because they are constantly included in team discussions, and so are aware of all findings as soon as they are uncovered. They will also be included in all discussions of proposed recommendations. Given this level of buy-in, it would be quite surprising if any objections were to be made to the final report.

And finally, one should not underestimate the positive impact of agile auditing on auditor turnover. The collaborative environment associated with this approach is more likely to give clients a positive opinion of the auditors providing them with recommendations. This more welcoming view is substantially different from the normal dread with which clients anticipate the arrival of auditors. Given the happier environment, team members may very well decide to prolong their careers as auditors.

Summary

In the auditing profession, auditors are generally seen as being a hindrance who are to be dealt with as expeditiously as possible, so that employees can get back to their regular jobs. Agile auditing is a useful tool for reversing this mindset, so that auditors are welcomed as useful consultants who can provide real value to a business unit's operations.

Agile auditing is an especially useful technique to apply in an uncertain environment. Since work activities are broken up into short-duration sprints, it is easy for an audit team to change direction mid-course to pursue a different target – as dictated by the circumstances. For this reason, an agile audit team may be assigned to work in lock-step with a management team that is setting up a new business initiative, to ensure that all new risks are appropriately addressed as operations are created or modified.

Glossary

A

Agile. A method of project management that employs the division of tasks into short phases of work and the frequent reassessment and adaptation of plans.

Audit. The process of evaluating evidence in order to reach a conclusion.

F

Facilitator. The individual who is responsible for the smooth functioning of an agile audit team.

P

Product owner. The individual who maintains the product backlog and sets audit priorities.

S

Sprint. A time-limited project in which an audit team completes a specific set of tasks.

Index